CALM

CALM

50 MINDFULNESS AND RELAXATION EXERCISES TO DE-STRESS AND UNWIND

DR. ARLENE K. UNGER

METRO BOOKS
New York

METRO BOOKS
New York

An Imprint of Sterling Publishing Co., Inc.
1166 Avenue of the Americas
New York, NY 10036

© 2017 Quarto Publishing plc
Quantum Books is an imprint of The Quarto Group

This publication is not intended as a substitute for medical or
psychotherapeutic advice, and readers are advised to consult a healthcare
professional for individual concerns and to check that the exercises are
suitable for their particular needs. The creators of the work and the
publisher cannot be held liable for any actions that may be taken as
a consequence of the information in this book.

ISBN 978-1-4351-6653-0

For information about custom editions, special sales,
and premium and corporate purchases, please contact Sterling
Special Sales at 800-805-5489 or specialsales@sterlingpublishing.com.

Manufactured in China by Toppan Leefung Printers Limited

4 6 8 10 9 7 5 3

sterlingpublishing.com

MIX
Paper from
responsible sources
FSC® C104723

CONTENTS

INTRODUCTION

Everyone wants to feel calm and happy … but few of us actually manage it. The truth is that we are just not equipped for the 21st century—it is too fast, too crowded, too 24/7. And the more stressed we become, the harder it is to find the quiet times and places that are essential to our well-being.

But it doesn't have to be this way. There are antidotes to the clamor, strain, and busyness of modern life, and there are means of breaking through the stress to achieve inner peace. You can find the answers in this book, which contains 50 different visualizations and exercises to help you to discover the calm we all crave.

What is calm?

Calm can be described as a state of mind where we are mentally and physically at peace with ourselves. It is a way of being that allows us not to overreact to feelings of anger or fear, to overwhelming problems, or to annoyance. It obviously involves not losing our temper, but it is more than that. Calm is a way of being in the world that helps us deal physiologically with daily stressors, and so it promotes good health.

Why physiologically? Because a mind that has been trained to be peaceful will stimulate the release of calming hormones. More specifically, our brains trigger the release of endorphins (happy hormones) when we are calm. This in turn lowers the level of cortisol (the stress hormone) in the body, resulting in feelings of tranquility.

So, while we can practice calming techniques in stressful situations, the goal is to make calm our normal, baseline state. This does not mean a life that is entirely without stress, or rising so far above problems that we ignore them. Rather, we can achieve calm when our mind and body are in tune with what is going on around us, but we are not constantly buffeted like a ship in a storm. Calm means cultivating a way of life based on balance, order, and harmony.

The enemies of calm

But why does calm matter all that much? Isn't it better to have a bit of excitement in life? Well, the opposite of calm is not excitement, it is stress. And there is a big difference between a little beneficial stress and a lot of out-of-control stress. Moreover, stress is not just an unpleasant feeling, it is also deeply damaging to our health and well-being.

When we are under chronic stress our body reacts by increasing our oxygen intake, our heart rate, and muscle tension. There is a sound reason for this: it is an ancient evolutionary reflex that prepares us to fight for our lives or run for the hills. But in modern life, the reaction triggered by stress is not usually accompanied by the heightened physical response that it is intended to enable. Our bodies get needlessly flooded with hormones, and that taxes our nervous system and drains our immune system. Chronic stress can lead to a range of physical and psychological ailments, from insomnia to heart disease to long-term anxiety and depression. This book draws on three methods that help combat stress and promote

When to seek help
Much of our stress can be resolved by self-help measures such as the ones outlined in this book. But if your emotional issues are continual, or they impact on your everyday life, relationships, or work, then consult your doctor or a professional therapist for individual advice and support.

10 BENEFITS OF CALM

Makes you feel happier

Restores good health and energy levels

Raises mental acuity and concentration

Inspires you to create and
enjoy yourself

Develops your intuition

Slows down the aging process

Helps you connect with yourself and build
better relationships with others

Enables you to relax, let go, and rejuvenate

Increases your capacity for hope,
forgiveness, and compassion

Allows you to spend more time on
what is important to you

calm: emotional brain training (EBT), cognitive behavioral therapy (CBT), and mindfulness-based stress reduction (MBSR).

Emotional brain training

In this therapy, mind-body interventions are used to address the stress reactions that undermine our ability to be calm. The tools of emotional brain training depend on the patient's reported brain state, which can range from "super calm" (level one) to "beyond stressed" (level five). There are also six "skills" that patients are encouraged to acquire. These include "setting effective limits" and "taking out the emotional trash"—that is, dumping bad feelings and past pain.

Cognitive behavioral therapy

This therapy holds that our thoughts, not external events, form the basis of our actions and feelings. If we can retrain our thoughts, we can control our reactions, rather than trying to change the people and stimuli around us. Cognitive behavioral therapy helps the patient to see that every thought is a hypothesis that can be questioned. Once that has been established, harmful reactions and behavior can be changed through tools such as journaling, list writing, distraction, and visualization.

Mindfulness-based stress reduction

Non-spiritual meditative and yoga-related teachings form the basis of this therapy. Mindfulness helps us to manage stress by attending to our breathing, feelings, thoughts, bodily sensations, and surroundings, without judgment. A key concept is "being in the moment." This simply means

Positive affirmations
Throughout the book you'll find a number of positive affirmations. These are short phrases that you can repeat in order to reinforce a message in your subconscious and which encourage you to develop positive perceptions of yourself.

allowing yourself not to be troubled by the past (which you cannot change) or the future (which has not happened). The only reality is the now; and if you can focus on that, then many of your regrets about the past and fears for the future will fall away.

This book shows you how to access a more serene state in your daily life by combining or sampling these three methods. None of the exercises takes more than a few minutes to do. But practiced regularly they have the power to transform your emotional state, and help you find a much greater sense of calm and well-being.

Below: By using visualization and other strategies, we can change our perspective and rise above needless stress and anxieties.

A DAY IN THE LIFE

A little stress can be a good thing. Our bodies are designed to deal with a certain amount of it, and it can help us to get motivated and to focus on what we need to do. But when we have too much stress, or if it is continual, then stress can make us miserable and deprive us of calm. It's a growing problem: more than 40 percent of American adults have experienced discomfort or illness that is due to stress. And some of those people turn to unhelpful ways of dealing with their stress, such as alcohol, which can make matters worse.

There are better, more positive ways of dealing with stress in our daily lives. We can learn to handle it when it arises and—just as importantly—we can find ways to release our minds and bodies from a negative cycle of stress, allowing them to relax fully. In this chapter you will find a variety of simple strategies to help you. Together they will help you to bring a greater sense of calm into your waking hours.

01 LET THE SUN SHINE

Get your day off to a positive start with this glorious sunlight visualization. Sunlight is a natural way to induce a calm state of mind, because it boosts levels of the feel-good hormone serotonin in the body. Paradoxically, when we are exposed to at least two hours of morning daylight, we tend to sleep better at night, which also helps us to regulate our moods.

1 As you awake in the morning, lie perfectly still for a moment. Breathe in and pay close attention to how it feels to hold in all that air. As you slowly exhale, imagine breathing out a brilliant gold light (this is easier with your eyes closed).

2 As you continue to breathe, visualize the golden light growing and growing, until it envelops your whole body and then spreads outward to fill the room.

3 Enjoy the sensation of being bathed in warm light, allowing yourself to feel vibrant and rested. Then open your eyes and get up slowly, vowing to bring as much light into your day as you possibly can.

WHEN TO DO IT

Practice this exercise for 5 minutes at the start of each day. Waking up with the sun on your mind will better prepare you to embrace natural light during the day.

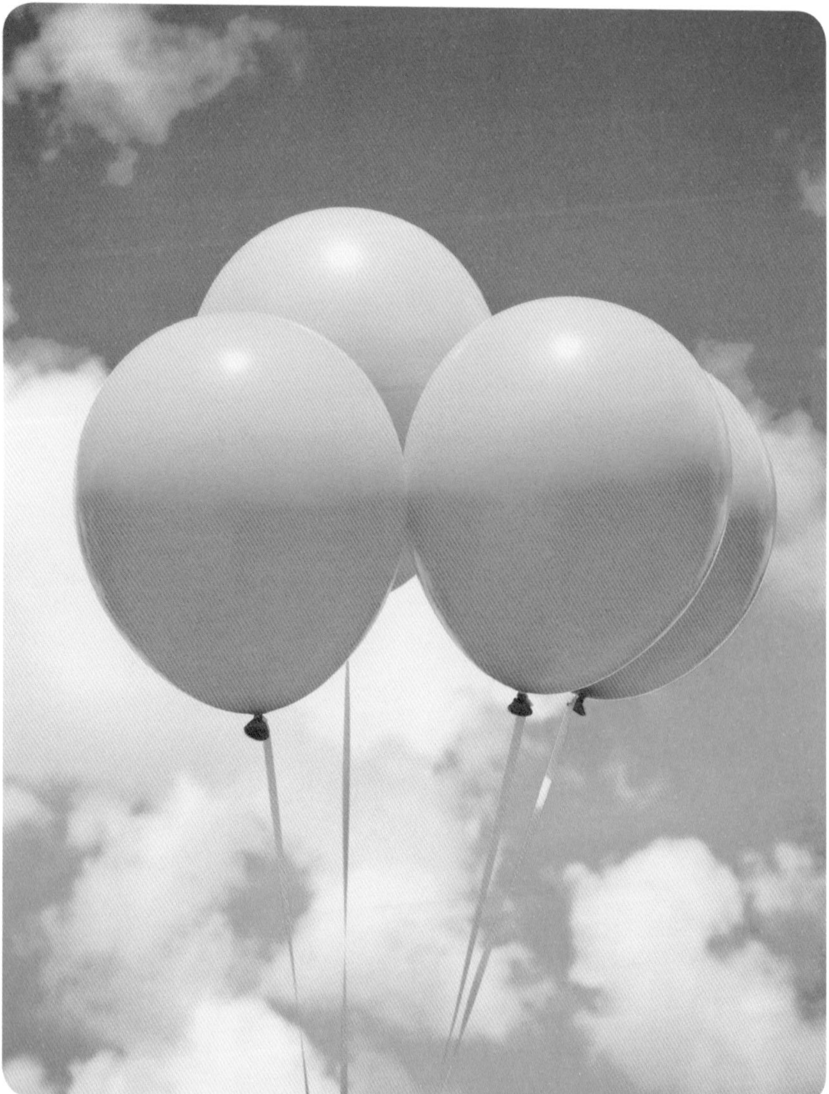

BALLOON BREATHING

When we are sitting at a desk or walking in the country, our thoughts are often far away—remembering, regretting, worrying, anticipating. Countless studies have found that paying attention to the present moment can help you to feel calmer and more in control. Try this mindfulness breathing exercise to bring yourself back to the moment at any time of day.

1 Sit in a chair and uncross your legs, placing your feet flat on the floor. Sit up reasonably straight.

2 As you close your eyes, take and hold in a big breath. Gently put both hands on your chest and imagine your lungs as a brightly colored balloon.

3 As you slowly exhale, visualize the balloon deflating. Then imagine it growing big again as you breathe in.

4 Keep filling and emptying your balloon, focusing on the feeling of expansion and contraction, until you begin to relax. If your busy mind wanders into the world of memos and memories, gently refocus it back on your balloon.

WHEN TO DO IT

Try doing this breathing exercise for a minute first thing in the morning and last thing at night. Over time, you will find it easy to build up to 5 minutes, 10 minutes, or longer.

03 PET TALK

If you are often self-critical, try this visualization to develop kindness toward yourself. Developing a nurturing inner voice is a key skill we learn in emotional brain training. The idea is that everyone has the ability to be self-nurturing, and this is essential if we are to achieve calmness.

1 Imagine the sweetest pet being your shadow all day and night—a dog or a cat, or any animal that takes your fancy (you can, of course, use your own pet if you have one). The main thing is that your pet loves and adores you.

2 When your pet is obedient, you generously praise it. If it does something naughty, you tell it so in a firm but still affectionate voice.

3 Before opening your eyes, decide that from now on you will talk to yourself the same way you would your imaginary pet.

WHEN TO DO IT

This is a good exercise to do for 5 minutes at the start of the day. By imagining talking to your "pet shadow" you can gradually train your nurturing voice to feel strong and genuine.

04 SMELL THE COFFEE

This mindfulness exercise is designed to open our eyes—and all our senses—to the pleasures of everyday life. We cannot be calm if we are always rushing from one thing to the next. Appreciating the small things can create tiny pauses in the day, which helps to engender an overall sense of calm and perspective.

1 On a piece of paper, make a list of the five senses —sight, smell, taste, touch, hearing. Leave a space between each heading.

2 Take the list with you when you leave the house. Try to notice an interesting stimulus for each of the senses: the smell of a coffee shop that you walk by, the color of a front door, the texture or temperature of a handrail, the taste of your chewing gum, the sound of a bird in the trees.

3 Stay aware until you have noted something under each heading, and can say that all your senses have been engaged. Try to keep this sense of engagement as you continue on your journey.

4 You might like to make a point of writing down your observations in a small notebook. You may be surprised at how diverting this challenge is, and at how fascinating it is to look through past entries.

WHEN TO DO IT

This is a great exercise to do every day on the way to work, and can transform a familiar journey that you may make on autopilot into a much more vibrant and fulfilling experience.

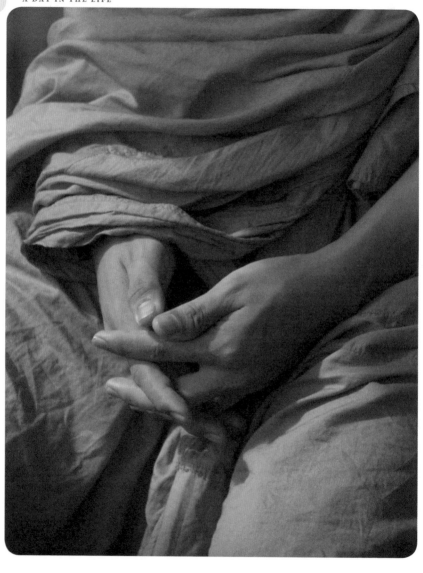

05 DRIVE WITH A MONK

Do you drive on autopilot or rage at others on the road? If so, this exercise is for you. Driving can easily disturb our equilibrium: the traffic tie-ups, lane-weavers, and freeway racers can lead us to feel agitated and distract us from the road. Mindful driving means being completely aware of how we're driving, the road conditions, and other people's driving habits without becoming overwhelmed by them.

1 When you sit down behind the wheel of your car, before you turn on the ignition, close your eyes and take three cleansing breaths. Imagine a friendly monk is sitting in the passenger seat.

2 Taking inspiration from your calm passenger, slowly and deliberately prepare to drive: open your eyes, put on your seat belt, check your mirrors, turn on the engine, release the hand brake, and move away. Your mind is completely still, but all your attention is entirely on the act of driving.

3 If along the way you encounter anything that disturbs your peace, imagine that you can hear the voice of your monk saying: "*Easy as you go. The journey is as important as the destination; you might as well enjoy the drive.*"

WHEN TO DO IT

Try this exercise every time you get in your car. Slowing your mind means a safer drive, and you will arrive at your destination feeling calmer and fresher.

HOW TO HELP

Use time spent at red traffic lights to appreciate a momentary pause: take one breath in and out, and relax your jaw, shoulders, and any other areas of tension.

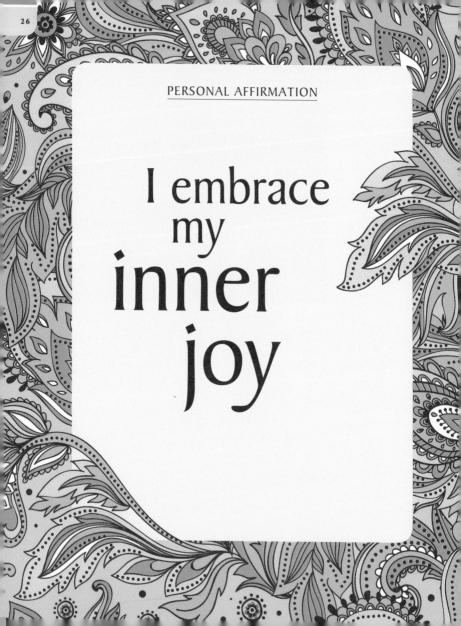

PERSONAL AFFIRMATION

I embrace my inner joy

06 LAUGH OUT LOUD

When we feel stressed, we tend to lose our sense of humor. But laughing is known to be good for our mental health. It reduces our levels of cortisol, the stress hormone, and releases endorphins, the body chemical that produces feelings of calm happiness. In emotional brain training, the ability to make ourselves smile is one of the ways we find inner joy—try this simple exercise to reconnect with yours.

1 Starting to laugh is like starting a fire. You need something to get it going—but once it catches it looks after itself. So begin by thinking of the funniest thing that ever happened to you, some incident that never fails to bring a smile to your lips.

2 Now "act" laughing out loud, as if you were in a play. Don't hold back (this is probably best not done on public transport). Throw yourself into the act of laughing, while keeping the funny memory in mind. Giggle, guffaw, hoot with laughter.

3 You will almost certainly find that your fake laughter turns into real laughter. Once that happens, keep it going. Laugh till you cry. You will feel so much better for it afterward.

WHEN TO DO IT

Laugh every morning—it can help to do it while you watch yourself in a mirror. Laughter is contagious, so try doing it with someone you live with.

LOVE YOUR CHORES

This exercise shows you how to turn even the dullest chore into a meditative experience that can reconnect you with feelings of calm and well-being. This is the message of mindfulness: that you can live a fuller and calmer existence if you embrace the present moment rather than wishing it was over or being distracted by thoughts of the past or future.

1 Begin by doing a typical chore around your home such as folding clothes, watering plants, or even emptying the dishwasher. Pay special attention to each step of the task. Tune into the smells, sounds, movements. Are there elements to this everyday task that you never noticed before?

2 Really focus on the sensual details: the smell of clean sheets, the gentle thudding of the tumble-dryer, the beauty of a droplet on a plant you are watering.

3 As you examine these new-found sensations, you may begin to notice that your thoughts are less random, that the carousel of worries and fantasies slows down, and that you are calmer than before.

WHEN TO DO IT

Try out this mindful activity with one daily chore. You will get better at it with practice, and the calming effect will grow stronger.

TOP **FIVE** WAYS
to de-stress in an instant

Go for a walk

Chat to a friend
or loved one

Visualize something
positive or hopeful

Put on some music
and dance

Take three deep
mindful breaths

08 SAY THANK YOU

If your day feels tricky, switch your focus and try this emotional brain-training exercise to access the powerful feeling of gratitude. Gratitude doesn't always arise spontaneously; it is something you can train yourself to feel. When you practice gratitude you are acknowledging the positive in your life, which can help you to feel more at peace with the way things are.

1 Think of something good about your day. It could be as simple as the hot shower you enjoy every morning, the beautiful flowers growing in your yard, or your loving relationship with your children.

2 Close your eyes and bring this thing to mind. Picture it in as much detail as you can, and silently say "thank you" for its presence in your life. Notice any sensations of gratitude that you feel.

3 Keep concentrating on your object or person for 30 seconds, allowing the feelings of gratitude to encompass you as you breathe naturally and calmly.

WHEN TO DO IT

You can do this exercise at any time of day, or try it in the evening when you get home from work. However hard your day has been, there is always something you can give thanks for.

09 DAILY PRACTICE

No-one can instantly convert unproductive living habits into productive ones. It doesn't happen overnight, and it is not always a smooth process. Inner calm is a skill that you have to nurture and develop over time—like learning a language or a musical instrument. Here are six useful habits to bring into your daily life.

1 Take time every day to notice the level of calmness in your life, body, feelings, and mindset. Rather than denounce or deny negative feelings, take a serious look at what you might not be doing for yourself in this regard.

2 Be aware of what is pulling and tugging at your life. What needs to stay or go? What steps can you take to ensure that this happens?

3 Structure your schedule to allow for more calm-producing activities. Think about what worked or didn't work for you in the past.

4 Realize the self-sabotaging things you do and say that keep you from feeling calm.

5 Fortify yourself with "positive self-talk" to help put you back on track quickly if you become overwhelmed or lose your temper. Getting upset with yourself just doesn't help.

6 Find support. Everyone needs people to keep them motivated toward positive strategies and to lean on when they hit obstacles. If you find emotional issues frequently getting in the way of your harmony, seek the help of a professional.

WHEN TO DO IT

Follow these steps as often as you can. It's also helpful to sit down and review your day each evening. Did you handle things the way you hoped or did you let your negative emotions get the better of you?

10 COLOR YOUR WAY CALM

Adult coloring has become hugely popular because it is both fun to do and is an easy way to unwind. When you color, you become wrapped up in what you are doing, and your mind disengages from repetitive or unhelpful thoughts. Try this simple exercise to get started.

WHEN TO DO IT

Any time you like! Coloring can be an enjoyable hobby, or you can use it to help you to manage feelings of anxiety or stress. It's a great activity to do in the evening, to soothe the mind into a relaxed state for sleep.

1 Find a quiet and comfortable place to color, and get all your coloring pens or pencils ready.

2 Try the coloring that follows. You can take a photocopy if you like, or you can color directly into the book (put a piece of paper behind the page if you are using felt pens or markers, so they do not bleed through).

3 Work at your own pace—there is no rush—and don't feel that you have to finish the coloring all in one go. Many colorists take a few days to do one design.

Turn the page: try the coloring exercise overleaf

BE GOOD
TO YOURSELF

One of the most straightforward ways to feel calmer and happier is to look after yourself. Emotional brain training and cognitive behavioral therapy both promote the benefits of a healthy lifestyle, because the first step to achieving a greater sense of calm is often to meet your physical needs. But the busier we get, the harder we find it to take the time to eat well, do the right amount of exercise, and get enough sleep.

A healthy lifestyle doesn't require working out like a demon or going on a raw-food diet—it means connecting with your body's needs, moment by moment, and developing good habits to replace the bad. It's long been proven that a nutritious diet and regular exercise can help to balance mood and reduce stress. This chapter offers a range of techniques designed to help you rebalance your attitude to food, overcome any reluctance to do health-giving exercise, and develop a kinder, more loving attitude toward yourself.

11   EATING MINDFULLY

If you tend to eat on the run or in front of the TV, try this exercise. Eating mindfully is essentially the process of focusing intently on how and what we are eating while savoring every moment of the experience. When we eat consciously, we enjoy our food more and we get the added benefit of staying calm. Mindful eating can help transform our relationship with food, which can often be a source of stress.

1 Get a juicy orange and place it before you. Focus on your breathing for a minute or so. When you feel relaxed, look closely at the orange. Examine the bright and fragrant fruit as if you've never seen one before. Attend to its color, the surface of the peel, and the shape of the fruit.

2 Now bring it up to your nose and smell the skin. Look for the best place to start peeling, and slowly and carefully peel off its skin, one piece at a time.

3 Once you have peeled your orange, pull the sections apart. Notice how they feel in your hands, and how they look and smell.

4 Place one of the segments in your mouth, but instead of biting and swallowing right away, allow your tongue to explore it for a while.

5 Feel its texture, then lightly puncture its skin with your teeth. Be aware of the squirt of juice and notice how it tastes in your mouth. Then slowly swallow just the juice, leaving the rest of the orange segment in your mouth.

WHEN TO DO IT

Once a day. Eating mindfully is a great way to avoid overeating or binge eating; it makes you much more aware of the size of your portions and slows down your eating, so that you notice when you are satisfied.

6 Now slowly chew the orange, and explore it with your tongue, noticing the taste in your mouth and how it changes as you continue to chew.

7 Swallow the rest of the orange, being aware of how it moves down your throat and how the taste lingers. Now eat the next segment in the same way. If you notice that you are suddenly lost in your thoughts, don't berate yourself, but simply bring your attention back to the sensations in your mouth.

HOW TO HELP

Make a point of eating your meals and snacks at a table rather than on the sofa or standing up at a countertop. It can help to have a short ritual before eating—saying a simple prayer, or by taking two deep breaths to allow yourself to mentally arrive.

8 Try to eat the rest of the orange with the same level of attention. When you finish, reflect on how this exercise felt—did you experience impatience or pleasure, or both.

9 Next time you eat, bring this exercise to mind and try to introduce a sense of mindfulness to your eating. It can help to take a few deep breaths before you start. You can also try the exercise with another food—some chocolate or a glass of wine.

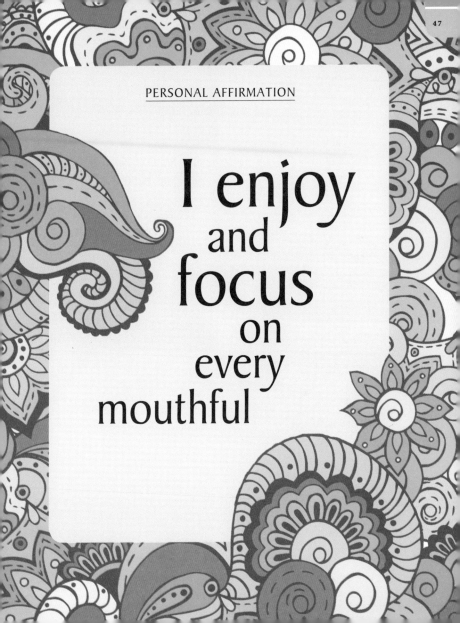

PERSONAL AFFIRMATION

I enjoy
and
focus
on
every
mouthful

12 FIT FOR PURPOSE

Exercise can be a great calming technique, but it can also be the last thing we feel like doing when we are tired or overwhelmed. In emotional brain training, we use inspiration and joy to counter resistance to positive change. Try these four ways to make the workout seem more appealing.

1 Get the clothes. If you feel good in your fitness gear, you'll be more likely to get out there.

2 Make a soundtrack. Listening to music that you love will help to make exercising a treat that you look forward to.

3 Join a group. Whether you want to run, bowl, swim, dance, or hike, it is more fun if you are doing it with other like-minded people; you are also more likely to turn up if you have an exercise buddy.

4 Set a goal. Try doing a charity walk, or run a mile, or swim 20 lengths—an attainable target can be a great motivator. You can make your aim public, or keep it to yourself. It's up to you.

WHEN TO DO IT

Aim to do everything on this list at least once over the next month. You'll see your attitude to exercise change for the better, and others will see a calmer you.

13 SIT ON A BENCH

It almost goes without saying that we need to give our mental faculties a rest from time to time. One of the simplest ways to do this is just to get out in the open—time spent outside can calm a preoccupied mind and teach us to find solace in nature. Try this beautiful mindfulness exercise.

1 Pick a quiet space where you can be still for a few minutes. It needn't be a perfect beach or a mountaintop: a bench in a park or your own back yard will do.

2 As you sit there, tune into your surroundings. Try to take note of everything that is within your field of vision: the plants and trees, any movements such as waving branches or scudding clouds, passers-by, birds, or insects.

3 Now narrow your attention to something very small: the woodgrain of the bench where you are sitting, a blade of grass, a pebble. Observe its shape, its color, its texture in detail. Then, as you breathe in, acknowledge just how much being in the outdoors brings you peace of mind.

WHEN TO DO IT

Try to do this exercise every day, without fail, for 10 minutes. Notice the space and quiet that downtime gives you. See how you are able to disconnect from hectic living, see the whole picture, appreciate the little things, and feel a sense of true calm.

Are there things that
I'd rather be doing than
what I am doing now?

*

What is preventing me
from doing the things I feel
are most important?

*

What areas of my life
am I neglecting?

*

Are there dreams
I have not realized; if so,
what are they?

14   TIME FOR NURTURE

How much time do you reserve to take care of yourself each day? If the answer is "not much" or even "none," try this exercise. It uses the cognitive behavioral therapy tools of scheduling and self-assessment to encourage you to find time for self-nurture. Time is the most important and loving gift we can allow ourselves in our quest for calm.

1 Thinking about the week ahead, use the planner overleaf to block off the time you will spend each day on different activities (work, socializing, eating, chores, family time, leisure). Use colored pencils, a different one for each activity; make a note of what each color represents at the top of the planner.

2 Look at the results. Does the activity you are spending the most time doing reflect what you really want from life or is there a disconnect? If you spend too much time at work, for example, are you robbing yourself of time you need for leisure? Or are you spending hours in front of the TV when you could be doing something more self-nurturing?

3 If so, set aside the time to reflect on the questions opposite. Noticing imbalances in your life is the first step toward correcting them.

WHEN TO DO IT

Make time to try this exercise at least once a week; you can photocopy the planner. This can help you to take better charge of your time, which can in itself help you to feel calmer.

Weekly planner

Work   Eating   Family Time   Sleeping

Socializing   Chores   Leisure

MONDAY

1am	2am	3am	4am	5am	6am	7am	8am

9am	10am	11am	12pm	1pm	2pm	3pm	4pm

5pm	6pm	7pm	8pm	9pm	10pm	11pm	12am

TUESDAY

1am	2am	3am	4am	5am	6am	7am	8am

9am	10am	11am	12pm	1pm	2pm	3pm	4pm

5pm	6pm	7pm	8pm	9pm	10pm	11pm	12am

WEDNESDAY

1am	2am	3am	4am	5am	6am	7am	8am

9am	10am	11am	12pm	1pm	2pm	3pm	4pm

5pm	6pm	7pm	8pm	9pm	10pm	11pm	12am

THURSDAY

1am	2am	3am	4am	5am	6am	7am	8am
9am	10am	11am	12pm	1pm	2pm	3pm	4pm
5pm	6pm	7pm	8pm	9pm	10pm	11pm	12am

FRIDAY

1am	2am	3am	4am	5am	6am	7am	8am
9am	10am	11am	12pm	1pm	2pm	3pm	4pm
5pm	6pm	7pm	8pm	9pm	10pm	11pm	12am

SATURDAY

1am	2am	3am	4am	5am	6am	7am	8am
9am	10am	11am	12pm	1pm	2pm	3pm	4pm
5pm	6pm	7pm	8pm	9pm	10pm	11pm	12am

SUNDAY

1am	2am	3am	4am	5am	6am	7am	8am
9am	10am	11am	12pm	1pm	2pm	3pm	4pm
5pm	6pm	7pm	8pm	9pm	10pm	11pm	12am

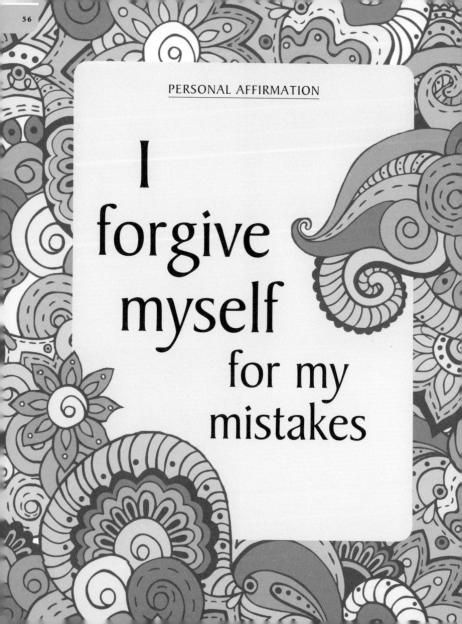

PERSONAL AFFIRMATION

I forgive myself for my mistakes

15 THE FRIEND WITHIN

We can get far angrier with ourselves than with others. But berating yourself boosts levels of the stress hormone cortisol, which leads to more anxiety. Try this emotional brain-training visualization when you are piling on the guilt; it will help you to find the friend within who can acknowledge and understand your mistakes, and allow you to let go.

1 Sit down facing an empty chair. Imagine that the chair is occupied by your closest friend, and that this friend is listening in on your thoughts.

2 Your loving, sympathetic friend knows that you have been beating yourself up about a mistake that you made earlier, and now they decide to speak to you about it. You hear them say that they know you are sorry and to stop dwelling on the error, that you will be OK.

3 As your friend speaks, you feel the wisdom of what they are saying. The guilt begins to lift, and a kind of serenity creeps back in. You silently repeat to yourself: "I forgive myself for my mistakes."

WHEN TO DO IT

Do this exercise daily for 5 minutes when you feel reasonably calm. Once you are familiar with it, you will find it much easier to do when you are feeling bad about yourself. By becoming a loving friend to yourself, you can put your inner critic to rest.

TOP **FIVE** WAYS
to nurture your body

Make getting enough
sleep a priority

Give yourself time
for a healthy breakfast

Get outside in the
fresh air every day

Stretch, do yoga, or practice
breathing exercises each evening

Treat yourself
to a long, hot bath

16 HEAR THE LOVE

If you struggle to feel happy about yourself, try this visualization, which draws on the emotional brain-training ideals of authenticity and self-love. Self-love isn't just about appreciating our "positives," it means accepting our whole being, flaws and all. This authentic self-acceptance gives us the inner equilibrium needed to stay calm.

1 Take a few cleansing breaths and close your eyes. Imagine that you are in a beautiful cavern. There is light, and the walls echo at any sound. You say "hello," and you hear the word echoed back to you in a warm voice.

2 Now think of someone that you love (it can be someone from your past or present life). In the cavern of your imagination, speak out loud all the things that you would like to say to that beloved, person: "I love you," "You are so special," or "I love you no matter what."

3 Hear these words lovingly echoed back to you. Continue to hear the echoes, and accept that these are meant for you.

WHEN TO DO IT

Practice this exercise every day, or whenever you are feeling bad about yourself. Mentally "hearing" your own thoughts repeated back to you can help you to gradually accept feelings of love for yourself.

17   LOSE THE CLUTTER

Keeping our surroundings free from clutter can help us to stay calm. Clutter is stressful—our brains get troubled and don't work as well when we are surrounded by muddle and untidiness. This is partly because the very idea of cleaning up is a cause of stress—you have so many more urgent things to do! Cognitive behavioral therapy encourages us to stop procrastinating, which helps us to feel less anxious as a consequence. So here is how to get the job done.

1 Zero in on one thing that is out of place, pick it up, and put it away. Then move on to the next thing. By tidying up one object at a time, you make steady progress. Try doing seven things before leaving for work.

2 Choose a small area to clear, such as a drawer or shelf, each day. Have two bags ready, one for things you want to dump, the other for things to give away.

3 Make a point of tidying as you go along. Keep countertops and tabletops clear rather than storing things here permanently.

4 Take out the trash every day, and make your bed soon after getting up. These simple habits can help you to start getting more organized.

5 Clean your windows regularly. It is amazing how much difference that makes to how your home looks and how you feel about it.

6 Once your place is tidy, try to keep it that way. Make it a rule that people should leave rooms as they found them.

WHEN TO DO IT

As often as you need to. It can help to get everyone in your home involved—since everyone makes the mess, this is only fair. Hire extra help if you need it; having a cleaner even once every two weeks can help you to get your home in order.

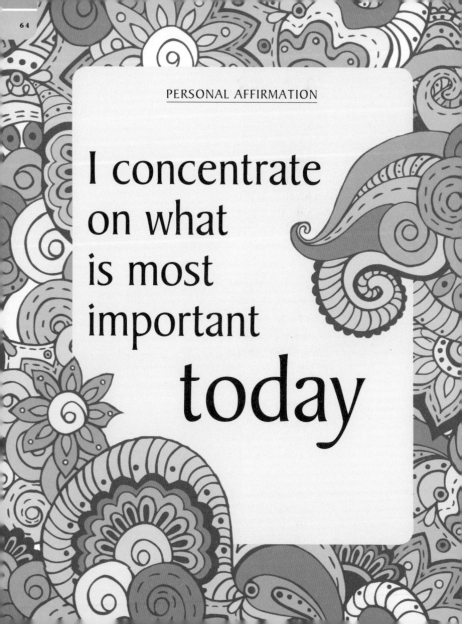

PERSONAL AFFIRMATION

I concentrate
on what
is most
important
today

18 MAKE A LIST

If you often wake up in the night feeling anxious—or struggle to drop off in the first place—try this list-making exercise, which is a technique used in cognitive behavioral therapy. It helps you to sort out what you should tackle first and what can wait. By prioritizing, we can regain a sense of control over our days, which can help us relax enough to allow us to sleep.

1 Take a piece of paper and rule it into three columns. You are going to sort all your tasks into three categories: column one, things that can't wait; column two, things that should be done sooner rather than later; column three, things that it would be good to get done eventually.

2 Assign your tasks to one column or another. When you have finished, look at column one: this is your to-do list for the next day. As for columns two and three, leave them for a different list on a different day.

3 If you find yourself feeling overwhelmed during the day, look at your list and use the affirmation opposite to help yourself focus.

WHEN TO DO IT

Do this exercise each evening just before bed to help you organize your priorities for the next day. Gradually you'll get better at seeing what is genuinely urgent and what isn't— which is sure to make for a calmer and more efficient working day.

19 | SLEEP LIKE A BABY

Getting enough sleep is essential for your mental well-being. If you have trouble falling asleep, apply the tools of cognitive behavioral therapy to restructure your thinking. Replacing self-defeating thoughts about sleep with positive mental images encourages your body to accept rest and your mind to dream freely.

1 As you lie awake in bed, try to stay perfectly still. Resist the temptation to toss and turn, or to flip the pillows.

2 Bring to mind a sleeping baby like the one in the picture. Focus on how profoundly peaceful that sleep is. Evoke in yourself the feelings of warmth and protection that a newborn naturally experiences while being held.

3 Now visualize putting your newborn to sleep. See yourself swaddling and gently rocking your new baby. Keep going until your eyes feel heavy enough to stay shut. Allow yourself to drift gently off to sleep.

WHEN TO DO IT

Repeat this exercise every night until just thinking about sleeping like a newborn puts you in the mood to drop off.

HOW TO HELP

Keeping a consistent bedtime, and getting up at the same time each day (including weekends), will also benefit your sleep.

20 DIVERT YOURSELF

If you turn to food, drink, or tobacco when stressed, try these ideas to deal more healthily with a build-up of tension. They are drawn from cognitive behavioral therapy, which is often used to help manage food addiction and cravings. It helps us extinguish unwanted behaviors by showing us how to distract ourselves away from unhealthy urges, and toward other activities.

WHEN TO DO IT

Whenever you find yourself craving something unhealthy. Food cravings are often about boredom—deal with the boredom, and you are more than halfway to managing an unhealthy craving.

1 Whenever you feel a sugar craving, take that as a signal to put yourself out of harm's way.

2 Put on your shoes and go for a walk—walking will put distance between you and the contents of your fridge. Put your earphones in: listening to music that you love will fulfill a need for stimulation and induce calm—or listen to a podcast, something factual and fascinating. Feeding your mind can be as satisfying as feeding your stomach.

3 If you can't get outside, then shift to a calming activity that helps you feel nurtured and nourished. Try writing to a friend, reading an inspiring book, or coloring.

Turn the page: try the coloring exercise overleaf

AN OASIS
AT WORK

Much of the recurrent stress that we experience comes from our jobs, or from trying to balance the pressures of our careers with our relationships, social scene, and home life. And it has never been harder to maintain a sense of perspective at work. It's become commonplace to work longer hours as workload pressures increase. Plus, digital advances mean we are always on call. Most of us cannot help checking our work mail when we wake up, and again through the evening when we are supposed to have left the office behind for the day. This prevents us from ever getting into relax mode.

The exercises in this chapter will help you to find time for yourself, however busy you may be. They will show you how to reconnect to calmness in an instant. And since many of us worry about our work performance, they also give practical strategies for improving efficiency. In the end, calm is more likely than stress to lead to greater productivity. Mindfulness, for example, improves our ability to concentrate and helps our memory to function—and so makes us more successful at work.

21 REACHING THE PEAK

This is a good visualization if you tend to work too hard or too long. Often, we think that there is something heroic about being the last to leave the office, or pulling an all-nighter to meet a deadline. But it is pointless to work that way. We should be able to reach our targets without doing ourselves harm. Calmness involves bringing perspective to our work goals.

1 Sit comfortably and close your eyes. Imagine that ahead of you is a beautiful mountain that you plan to climb. Its summit seems a long way off.

2 At first the path up is manageable, but it quickly grows steeper and soon you are not walking but climbing—you grow tired and thirsty, but the peak seems no closer than it ever was.

3 So you change your approach. Instead of looking up at the mountain, you concentrate on each foothold and each moment, one at a time. You become so absorbed that you don't think about the goal. Then you remember the mountain and look up; the peak is so much closer. You feel you could reach out and touch its beautiful face.

WHEN TO DO IT

Practice this visualization for 5 minutes each morning. If you find yourself being overwhelmed by a gigantic task, bring the mountain to mind and remind yourself to take it one step at a time.

22   LET YOURSELF BLOOM

Everyone who has to face an audience struggles with nervousness. The key is to banish the false idea that you are bound to mess things up. That is not helpful (or true). This exercise will help you change your negative attitude toward your abilities.

1 Bring a flower to mind. It is a beautiful shape and color (any color you like), but it is closed tight. As you breathe, bring the flower closer and closer toward yourself until you and the flower are one. As the flower, you notice that you want to open up your petals, to display yourself in all your glory.

2 As you continue to breathe, imagine a warmth— the first rays of the rising sun. The dawn breaks, the head of the flower naturally relaxes. The petals spread wide, and the flower-head takes on its true daytime shape, and it is spectacular. Enjoy the sensation of being open and free.

3 Notice that all it took was for the time to be right. In the end, you, the flower, did what came naturally. The same is true of you, of the way you present your ideas and your personality.

WHEN TO DO IT

Try this exercise whenever you are nervous about talking or presenting to a group of people. It can help you to stay calm, and keep your mind centered on your message.

23 FIND A BALANCE

For decades, busy working people have struggled to divide their time between work and home, career and family, providing for their kids and actually being with their kids… Cognitive behavioral therapy can provide us with tools that allow us to see the issues more clearly, and perhaps get closer to the ideal balance. This simple exercise is a good place to start.

1 Take a blank sheet of paper and, with a ruler, draw a line vertically down the middle.

2 Write down on the left-hand side the things you feel are vital to the happiness of your life. These might be small things like being there to do the school run, enjoying a regular date night, or making it to a weekly yoga class.

3 On the right, note the things interfering with your happiness. Perhaps the untidiness of the kitchen depresses you, or your commute is too tiring.

4 The simple act of writing down the good and bad will give you clarity, and open the way to change. If a possible solution comes to mind, take steps to make it happen.

WHEN TO DO IT

Look at your two lists several times over the course of a week, and ask yourself what you could do: for example, put family occasions in the diary, so they don't get shunted aside; negotiate a regular home-working day, if possible; hire someone to clean for you.

a little nothing time makes me happy

24 MAKE ZERO TIME

Burn-out happens when our emotional output exceeds what we get back emotionally. If you knock yourself out at work, but feel unfulfilled, unappreciated, and isolated, then sooner or later you are going to grind to a halt. This exercise is designed to allow you to manage your inner resources. The key is to make time each day when you can replenish yourself by doing nothing.

1 Take a few deep breaths and pick up your calendar. Look over your past week—if it has been chock-full of tasks and appointments, vow to make the coming week different.

2 Pick up a pen and, instead of first filling in your "to-dos," ink in a time each day to do absolutely nothing. It is worth doing this on paper rather than on an electronic scheduler, which is easy to change.

3 When a task comes in, or someone wants to arrange a meeting, resist the temptation to do it in one of your zero times. Say you are busy—and mentally think: "I am busy doing nothing!" Use the affirmation opposite to remind yourself why you are doing this.

WHEN TO DO IT

Try this exercise when you are feeling depleted and unenthusiastic about life. You will learn that a little you-time can make you happier and more productive overall.

TOP **FIVE** WAYS
to have a healthier work day

Walk around
as you take a call

Switch off your email alert and
check your inbox at set times

Take a deep
breath before meetings

Keep water on your desk
and sip it throughout the day

Have breaks when
you need them

25 ELASTIC THOUGHTS

It can be hard to stay focused at work when we are bombarded with emails, calls, and people coming into our workspace. But our thoughts and worries can interfere with our work even more than all the external distractions. Mindfulness teaches us that interruptive thoughts are actually very pliable and, like elastic bands, can be pinged out of the way.

1 Close your eyes, and keep your attention on your breathing. Take several mindful breaths.

2 Picture your distractions as rubber bands that are making your desk untidy. Pick up one of them, and snap it to the back of your mind, saying: "We're at work now, we can think about this later."

3 Take a couple of breaths, then repeat the process a few times, until your desk is clear of distractions. Then open your eyes and bring your attention to work; if an interruptive thought comes to mind, simply visualize snapping it away.

WHEN TO DO IT

Try this visualization every day for two weeks, until it comes easily to you; then use it as you need to. If you have a recurring thought that is particularly hard to chase away, then make a mental note to address the issue later. It can help to make an "appointment" with your worry—decide to think about it at 5pm, for 20 minutes, say.

26 BUTTERFLY MIND

One instant way to gain more calm in your life is to stop multitasking. Research shows that when we try to multitask, the brain is simply switching from one activity to the other—it's less efficient and more stressful than attempting to do just one thing at a time. When you are next tempted to multitask, try this beautiful visualization.

1 Close your eyes and imagine that you are in a wildflower meadow. Fantastical butterflies, of every shape, size, and color, fill the air. You have a net and you want to capture one of these beautiful creatures, just to look at it for a moment.

2 You try to net a butterfly—any butterfly—in flight, but they are too swift and nimble. You paw at the air with your net, but can't come close. So you change tactics. You focus on one glorious blue butterfly that is resting on a plant. You screen out all the others—that technicolor blizzard of wings.

3 Suddenly the task is easy. You do no more than lay your net over the resting butterfly, as if you were covering it with a delicate blanket. Once you have admired its beauty, you release it into the sky.

WHEN TO DO IT

Spend 5 minutes doing this visualization before you leave for work. It will help you to keep the advantage of single-tasking at the forefront of your mind.

I protect myself and radiate positivity

27 BE YOUR BEST SELF

Maintaining a calm demeanor at work isn't always easy. Emotional brain training helps us to feel steadier by teaching us the importance of integrity. The key is to be ourselves and not allow others to contaminate our feelings of self-worth, our relationships, or our productivity. Here are four ideas.

1 Try seeing your place of employment as a living entity, made up of a random collection of personalities. People will always have issues, and, like viruses, these can be catching. Resolve to protect yourself by avoiding negativity and trying to reframe problems as opportunities.

2 When talking to others at work, try to stick with the facts, put feelings aside, and watch the delivery of your message. If you find yourself speaking harshly, pause and take a breath.

3 Make a point of smiling. This helps to relax the face, and can alter your brain and body chemistry. Smiling can also have a positive effect on the way people react to you.

4 Support your team members. Know that negativity can ricochet back to you.

WHEN TO DO IT

Every day! Having a positive attitude at work can prevent you from being sucked into other people's difficulties and issues, and help you maintain a sense of calm.

28 INSTANT SERENITY

If you are always on the go, then use this mindfulness-based exercise to give you a quick route to peace. When we allow ourselves to have a moment of calm, our mind relaxes and we restore our emotional endurance. Research has shown that over time mindful meditation can change our thinking patterns and help us bounce back from stress.

1 Sit or lie down somewhere comfortable, with your legs and arms uncrossed. Close your eyes.

2 Summon up an image that, for you, represents peace. It could be anything: the interior of a church or temple, a white unicorn, a coral reef, a forest glade, or a beautiful lake.

3 Spend some time sketching in the detail of that image in your mind's eye—for example, if you have chosen a forest glade, then imagine the color and texture of the tree trunks, the shapes of the leaves, the sunlight filtering through the canopy.

WHEN TO DO IT

Try this exercise at the same time each day—perhaps just before you leave for work. You can also do it if you need a well-deserved break—while sitting at your desk or on a train or bus.

4 As you slowly inhale, think of that peaceful place or object, and each time you exhale, say the word "peace" silently to yourself (or out loud if you are somewhere private). Do this a few times.

5 Now place one hand on your chest and the other on your abdomen, and repeat the breathing and speaking. Can you feel the measured beat of your heart, or notice the slow release of the tension in your abdomen?

6 Continue to breathe for a few moments, allowing your body to relax. When you feel ready, open your eyes slowly and take a couple more deep breaths before returning to the task at hand.

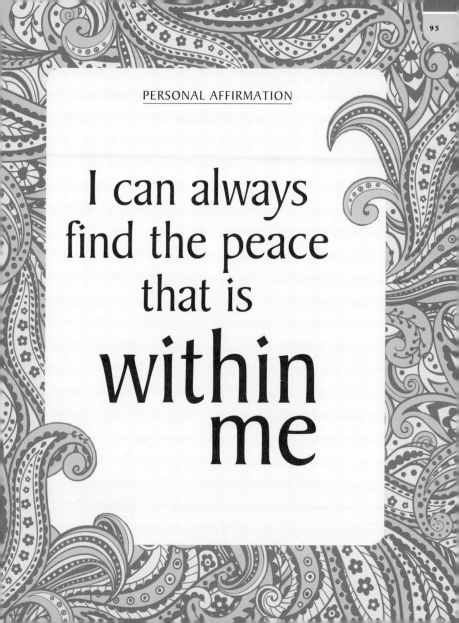

PERSONAL AFFIRMATION

I can always find the peace that is within me

29 MINDFUL MANDALA

If you find it hard to unwind, try decorating a mandala, a centuries-old spiritual symbol that is often used in art therapy and as a form of calming meditation. There is something about the symmetrical perfection of a circle that is particularly soothing to color.

WHEN TO DO IT

Coloring is a great stress-reliever. Give it a go during your lunch break, or when you get home in the evening. It's a more positive way to de-stress than slumping in front of the TV.

1 Before you start, get all the pens and pencils that you need ready. Have a few moments to center yourself. Take a few deep, calm breaths in and out, letting your shoulders drop and jaw unclench. Check that you are sitting comfortably.

2 Use your pens or pencils to color in the mandala design opposite. Let your instinct guide your choice of colors—there is no right or wrong. If you feel the need to free yourself from making a decision—even a tiny one—close your eyes and pick a pen or pencil at random. This can be very freeing.

3 Allow yourself to enjoy the process without worrying about the outcome. Try to carry that sense of calm through to the rest of your evening.

Try this: coloring a mandala can help you unwind

A
RESILIENT
MIND

Our feelings and thoughts can be stormy, and they can sometimes leave us washed up on some unhappy shore, like an emotional shipwreck. But it is possible, through meditation and other techniques, to plot a course to stiller waters, to a haven of peace.

Cognitive behavioral therapy and emotional brain training allow us to identify unhelpful ways of thinking that are causing us upset or imbalance. These methods show us that our thoughts and emotions have a huge impact on the way we behave—and they give us the means to alter harmful mental habits. The fact is that your mind can be trained to be peaceful; it is a knack that you can learn. Calmness is not just a question of keeping your temper on a leash. It goes much deeper than that. It is a different way of operating in the world; one that equips you to deal with stress, and helps to protect you from the harm that stress can cause on a physiological level.

30 FLOWER POWER

For most of us, life is a race. Slowing down is a mindfulness concept that helps us use our time wisely. We need reminders to encourage us to slow down. That's how this exercise works—it is a visual trigger to help you find the pause in a busy day.

1 Take 2 minutes to sit down in a comfortable chair. Close your eyes and picture a field of daffodils. Use your imagination to inspect the warm yellow hue, their nodding heads, how they glisten in the morning sun. Take time to really look: those gorgeous flowers are not going anywhere.

2 Before opening your eyes, fix an image of that captivating scene in your mind. Realize that the daffodils are there to gently remind you to slow down today. Bring the scene to mind whenever you feel yourself rushing.

WHEN TO DO IT

Make this short interlude an integral part of your morning routine—it's no more time, after all, than it takes to brush your teeth.

HOW OFTEN

As frequently as you like! The more often you do it the better it works. Keep a vase of flowers on your desk as a further reminder.

31 DRIFT AWAY WORRIES

We all fret about things outside our control. This emotional brain-training exercise involves visualizing your worries as something as insubstantial as a cloud, helping you understand that worries, like clouds, slowly change shape and fade away.

1 Lie comfortably and gaze at the ceiling. Imagine that you are staring at a blue sky flecked with a few white clouds. A worry is like a cloud seen from a distance. It seems to have density and form, but when you examine it closely it is mostly air, and it drifts away before your eyes.

2 With this image of clouds before you, say to yourself: "This too shall pass." Keep repeating the phrase to yourself: "This too shall pass; this too shall pass."

3 Now imagine the clouds are floating away. Once they drift out of sight, all you are left with is a sunny blue sky. Take a few moments to breathe and then get up slowly.

WHEN TO DO IT

If you are under ongoing stress, do this exercise before you get out of bed in the morning.

HOW OFTEN

Once a day at least—more often if you are able to take a few minutes to lie down during the day.

32 COUNT YOUR BLESSINGS

When we feel grateful, we can't help but feel more peaceful. Gratitude helps us to see things more positively, participate in activities more fully, and experience the value of life, all of which increase our feelings of calm and satisfaction. In cognitive behavioral therapy, journaling is used as a tool to help us keep track of all our reasons to be glad. Here's how to do it.

1 Do your journal at the same time each day. This helps you to make a habit of it.

2 Pick a number of thankful moments or incidents that you will write about each day. Three is a good number—not too few, not too many.

3 Write about things you savor: a spectacular sunrise, hiking in the hills, a loved one's smile, the affection of a pet, the music of a great street musician, a problem solved, or a trouble that has melted away.

4 Don't expect to remember everything. When some occasion of gratitude happens in the course of the day, get out your phone and mail it to yourself as an enjoyable reminder.

WHEN TO DO IT

Every day, before bedtime. Once a week, choose one instance of gratitude and expand on it, describing it and what it means to you more fully.

33 FLYING HIGH

Some people are always thinking of the worst-case scenario, and probably each one of us does it from time to time. But "catastrophizing" can get us riled up to the point that it wipes away our inner sense of calm. This useful exercise draws on the cognitive behavioral therapy tool of "pairing opposites," to help us break through pessimistic thinking.

1 Catch yourself when thoughts of hopelessness, gloom, dejection, or pessimism come over you. Try not to block those thoughts or to analyze them.

2 Instead, think two very positive thoughts: for instance, I am on top of the world; I am keeping the faith; I am on the crest of the wave; I am flying through the sky.

3 Make it a habit to outnumber negative thoughts with positive ones by a factor of two to one. Now you are ready to move on to the task at hand.

WHEN TO DO IT

Practice this exercise as often as you need to. Gradually you'll stop expecting the negative, and be more able to embrace the reality of daily life.

34 LET PETALS FALL

This mindfulness exercise is useful if you find it hard to relinquish control. We all like to believe that we are in command of our lives. But with that belief can come a fear that if we relax for a moment, everything will fall to pieces. Learning to welcome each moment without forcing a preconceived outcome is a key concept of mindfulness.

1 Imagine that you are in a walled garden, looking at the head of a flower. The flower is beautiful beyond words: you want it to stay that way forever.

2 But a breeze washes over the garden. The flower that you are looking at sways back and forth. No harm comes to it, but you realize that some time soon the wind will pick up, and the petals will fall off.

3 You return to your contemplation of the flower, paying close attention to the beauty of each petal. Your feeling of appreciation is all the greater, because you know that the flower's beauty will pass.

WHEN TO DO IT

Every day for 5 minutes. Remind yourself that letting things happen doesn't mean that you don't care, or that you have given up, but rather that you acknowledge that total control is an impossible and unhelpful aspiration.

35 A PLACE OF PEACE

If you want to feel calm, you can begin by creating a calming atmosphere around yourself. Listening to serene music, reading enriching literature, or looking at great art—even on the pages of a book—can evoke a sense of tranquility. You can also conjure up a mental image of peace by trying this emotional brain-training exercise. It is a visualization aimed at awakening the image-based part of your emotional brain.

1 Sit in a comfortable chair with your eyes closed; make sure that you are somewhere quiet and will not be disturbed. Take a minute to breathe quietly, allowing your body to relax as you do so.

2 Picture yourself looking up at the bluest of blue skies. You are barefoot on the sand dunes, and you can feel the sand beneath your toes. There are some tall grasses fringing the beach, and you reach out and touch them.

3 You can hear the gentle sound of waves, and you sit for a minute, enjoying the peace. Then you walk toward the sea across sand that is warm and yielding under your feet.

WHEN TO DO IT

Practice this exercise daily. See how your mind enjoys creating beautiful, soothing images when life is maddening and frantic. You can bring your "place of peace" to mind at stressful moments during the day for an instant self-soother.

HOW TO HELP

You may like to have a
soundscape to listen
to when you do this
meditation—a track
featuring the sounds
of the ocean is a
natural way to block
out distracting noises
and help you relax.

4 You come to the water and notice the aroma of
the ocean spray. Tempted, you walk into the
shallows, where the cool, refreshing water laps over
your toes.

5 You go further into the water, finally submerging
yourself to enjoy a refreshing swim and tasting
the salt on your lips.

6 When you emerge, you find a towel on the
beach for you to dry yourself with. It's thick, soft,
and warm from the sun. You then sit on the sand,
feeling utterly content and relaxed, watching the
gentle waves lapping in and out.

7 Continue to enjoy this sense of peace and
contentment as you slowly come out of the
visualization. Open your eyes, and take a couple of
deep breaths before getting on with your day.

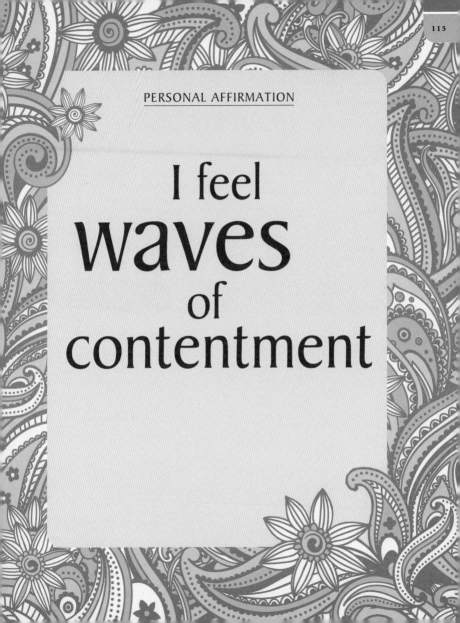

PERSONAL AFFIRMATION

I feel
waves
of
contentment

senta en tamaño natural...
detalles de esta linda...
anchos y tres matice...
cálices y los tallos son...
punto, cuyo largo varía s...
una aguja que tenga el ojo...
Cordón de seda y cinta de reps malv...

84. Traje con recogidos en abanico. — Este vestido... de fa...
de seda negra, con fondo de falda recabierto á plano por dela... con la...
de encina, entre los recogidos, que llevan un paño de 4 m. de... ho, asegu...
en 50 cent. en los bordes del lado. Se dispondrán los pliegues... rriba segú...
el dibujo 84. Se fruncirá por detrás. Se abrocha el cuerpo p... delante baj...

36 PICTURE YOUR DREAMS

We may think daydreaming is a waste of time, but there's evidence to show that focusing on our daydreams can have a calming effect on our psyche. What is more, many life-coaches and behaviorists believe that envisioning our dreams, or giving them some concrete form, makes them more attainable in life. This exercise, drawn from cognitive behavioral therapy, asks you to create a "vision board" as an affirmation of your dreams.

1 Get a cork board, a scrapbook, or a large piece of plain card stock or poster board—something on which you can arrange and re-arrange pictures.

2 Look in magazines for pictures or phrases that inspire you. Cut them out and keep them. Use your own drawings, colorings, or photos too.

3 Once you have a good collection of material, create your mood board. It should amount to a composite picture of your hopes, a collage of inspiration and aspiration. You might like to frame it or display it somewhere you will see it every day.

WHEN TO DO IT

Create your vision board over a period of about two weeks. Gradually your dreams will come into focus, creating the opportunity for you to pursue them in a spirit of calm determination.

37 PAY IT FORWARD

One way to access a calmer state of mind is to focus outward rather than inward. This exercise is based on the concept of "paying it forward." The idea is that you acknowledge the good that is done to you, and you pass that good on to someone else. Paying it forward helps build a sense of appreciation and community.

1 As you stand in front of your mirror in the morning, think about a kind act from which you have benefited—perhaps someone gave you a lift when it was raining, or a colleague helped you solve a problem at work. Take a moment to say a mental thank you.

2 Make a note to pay that kindness forward at some point in the day. You don't need to do a favor for the same person who did a good thing for you; if possible, pass the baton of kindness on to someone new. Perhaps you can buy the coffees, or help a frazzled parent get their stroller off the bus. Notice how good a small charitable act can make you feel.

WHEN TO DO IT

Make a point of doing this exercise every day for 30 days, and see it work its magic on the people around you.

38 CYCLE THROUGH DOUBT

This is a good visualization to do if you are indecisive. Emotional brain training teaches that the brain likes to fight with itself because it finds this preferable to uncertainty. That inner debate can be highly stressful, but a creative thought may pop up now and then. Noticing that thought and letting it propel you to action is the key to breaking the stand-off.

1 Visualize yourself on a leisurely bike ride in the countryside, enjoying pedaling past beautiful fields and meadows, hills and valleys.

2 Suddenly the terrain changes. You find yourself on the edge of a steep and winding downward path that is strewn with rocks. You can see that down below, beyond this scary descent, the way forward is green and even—but can you get there?

3 You decide to brave it. You freewheel quickly down the steep hill, trying hard to dodge the sharp and dangerous rocks. Amazing as it seems, you come to no harm along the way—in fact, you find it exhilarating—and when you reach the sunny flatlands at the bottom you are proud of yourself.

WHEN TO DO IT

Practice this visualization once a day for 5 minutes. Gradually you will see your self-doubt disappear and notice how your ability to take action when action is needed increases.

TOP **FIVE** WAYS
to build good mental health

Keep a gratitude journal

Use positive affirmations
that you can believe in

Acknowledge
your strengths

Forgive yourself
your mistakes

Remember how you
overcame difficulties in the past

39 GROW GREEN

This evocative visualization can be useful if you are feeling discontented or stuck in your life. It draws on the emotional brain-training concept of vibrancy, which is used to promote emotional centeredness. Vibrancy is about our ability to feel alive, to breathe life into what we have now, and to learn new things no matter where we are.

1 Before turning off the lights at night, sit up and close your eyes. Imagine waking up tomorrow and discovering that everything that you touch turns a brilliant emerald color. Even things that once looked old and tarnished are now growing and have turned a glorious, radiant green.

2 Add a lovely fresh aroma to all the greenery that now surrounds you. Breathe in all the fresh scents of mint, pine, ferns, spruce, or eucalyptus.

3 This is the new inner scenery that goes with you everywhere. It is a reminder that no matter how stagnant life may seem, there is always something to learn, enjoy, and imbibe.

WHEN TO DO IT

Every day for a week. Repeatedly doing this exercise can help you understand the importance of emotional growth and well-being regardless of where life is taking you.

40 DIAL DOWN FEELINGS

If you often let your emotions get the better of you, then dialing down can be a useful technique to learn. It involves identifying the intensity of an uncomfortable feeling and imagining that you are reducing it to a more manageable level.

1 If you notice yourself feeling angry or upset, then stop and pay attention to the quality of the emotion and how it feels within your body.

2 Give your feeling a rating of between one and eight—with one representing a feeling that is barely noticeable and eight being the most intense.

3 Label the feeling—say to yourself, for example, "I am feeling disappointed and I'm at a three." Keep observing the feeling, and notice how its intensity lessens once you label it.

WHEN TO DO IT

Try doing this exercise once a day, ideally when you are feeling reasonably calm. If you practice it regularly, you will find it easier to do when you are in the grip of a strong emotion, and can use it as an effective way to manage your emotions.

41 CALM THE STORM

Even if we have learned to bring a thread of calm into our daily routine, we can find it hard to keep our cool when faced with the unexpected disasters and upsets that are a part of every life. Is it possible to stay calm in the midst of an uncontrollable storm of emotion? One answer lies in mindfulness-based stress reduction, which offers us a range of tools that we can use when things seem to be falling apart. Try these useful strategies, either separately or in sequence.

1 Cast yourself as an onlooker who is curious, concerned, but not deeply involved. Adopting the attitude of an interested observer can help you to maintain a sense of perspective.

2 Put distance between yourself and your emotions. Rather than saying "I am panicking," say "I can feel panic in me." This helps you remember that panic will rise, subside, then pass, while you remain the same; remind yourself that you are not defined by transient emotions.

3 Acknowledge your needs. Ask for help if you need it. The people who love you will want to help you through hard times, so be open to them and to their wisdom.

4 Distract or console yourself. Engage in some kind of nurturing activity, such as deep breathing, meditation, or coloring.

5 Evoke positive memories. Reflect on your successes, recalling your earlier experiences of getting through tough times, and remembering what you learned.

Turn the page: try the coloring exercise overleaf

WHEN TO DO IT

Spend 15 minutes a day practicing these strategies for at least two weeks. Gradually, you'll recover your calm and get back in control of yourself.

CALMER
CONNECTIONS

Our relationships with others are crucial to our well-being. There is lots of evidence showing that quality time with family and friends promotes calmness and increases our sense of security. Spending good times with positive people can reduce our anger, boost our patience—and even increase our tolerance for pain.

So it is ironic that the people who bear the brunt of our stress, the ones we get angry with when it is all too much, are the people who are closest and most dear to us. This is natural but it is dangerous, because it creates a vortex of stress, arguments, and recrimination that can—if unchecked—damage or destroy our relationships.

So here are some ways to build a healthy pause into your interactions, to create better communication channels (both verbal and emotional) and to maintain inner peace even in difficult moments, when those around you are not the support that you might hope them to be. Love can be a source of calm; and calm can be an expression of love.

42 RIPPLES OF EMOTION

This is a useful exercise if you find yourself taking out your frustration on a loved one. A lot of us don't know what to do with our feelings. When we experience sadness or anger, we try to push it away, to distract ourselves, or to deny its presence. But when we allow ourselves to experience our emotions fully, we notice that they ebb and flow quite naturally, like an ocean tide. This can help us to maintain calmer connections.

1 Sit down, close your eyes, and take some deep breaths. As you breathe, imagine the bluest, calmest ocean you have ever seen. Picture yourself walking into the warm water: everything is OK.

2 Gentle waves start to wash toward you, and you're having fun meeting each new wave with a new breath. They become larger and larger. Then, suddenly, a huge wave engulfs you.

3 You are scared, but you have no choice but to allow it to wash over you, even toss you about. So you surrender to the wave. And slowly the power of the wave lessens and the sea is calm again. You may have initially felt scared but now you've been through it and feel proud of yourself.

WHEN TO DO IT

Try this visualization exercise when you feel upset and don't quite know where the feeling may be coming from. Its message is that we can maintain our inner sense of calm when we ride with the emotional wave. Surrendering to your feelings can be your best defense against a cycle of negative emotions.

I replace feelings of hurt with

compassion

43 BURY THE HATCHET

Holding a grudge is like being a prisoner to your anger. If you are harboring resentment, try these tools from cognitive behavioral therapy to restructure your thinking and let go of past wounds. It's good for your well-being, according to the Stanford University Forgiveness Project, which found that people who can forgive tend to have better immune systems and are more positive thinkers.

1 Know the meaning of forgiveness. It is not about justifying or excusing, but allowing the memory to fade naturally from the forefront of your mind.

2 Narrate your emotions. Express in words how you feel; do not vent your upset on others.

3 Create a framework. Think about why the hurt occurred. Finding a rational explanation can help to release some of the anger.

4 Feel safe. Think of what you can do to ensure your safety—do you need an apology or assurances from the person?

5 Don't be a victim. Resolve to stop dwelling on past hurt, and start living.

WHEN TO DO IT

Try these five steps daily for no less than 15–20 minutes. See how over time you become more spontaneous, calm, and optimistic.

44 CALL A HALT

If you struggle to say "no," then this visualization, inspired by cognitive behavioral therapy, can help you to become more assertive. Many of us find it hard to say "no" because we worry about causing conflict or hurt feelings. But an unwilling "yes" can cause more emotional distress than being straightforward. Here's how to feel positive about the negative.

1 Visualize a busy intersection in a crowded city. Something is wrong: there are no road markings, no traffic lights, no stop signs or crossings. The traffic is snarled up, horns are blaring, tempers are fraying; you even see cars bumping into each other as they jockey for position.

2 You blink, and as if by some magic all the necessary road furniture appears: the cars sort themselves into lanes, the red and green lights make the traffic flow, the cacophony of car horns disappears. You see that it is these restrictions and limits on traffic that make it possible for everyone to move forward.

3 Sit for a few moments, breathing calmly, as you resolve to say "no" when you want to.

WHEN TO DO IT

Try this exercise whenever you feel the need to remind yourself that the red light is not always obstructive.

HOW TO HELP

Simply saying "no, I can't do that" with a smile is often simpler than coming up with an excuse.

TOP **FIVE** WAYS
to have happier relationships

Let go of
old grudges

Really listen to what
the other person says

Make the first interaction
of the day a happy one

Remind yourself of the positives
this person brings to your life

Don't expect anyone to provide
everything you need

45 THE VOLCANO HEART

Romance can be wonderful, but it can also cause heartbreak. This visualization is useful if you are dealing with feelings of rejection or grief. In emotional brain training, we acknowledge that the process of emotional healing is like recovering from a physical injury: it takes time, care, and space. We need to fully experience the depth and the volcanic force of our emotions in order to move through devastation and find hope again.

1 Start by closing your eyes and concentrating on your breathing. Let the things that you are feeling rise up like magma inside an active volcano.

2 Don't hold back. Allow each emotion to gush out of the volcano. Your feelings are like rivers of lava: they are hot and searing, and they have a momentum of their own.

3 But notice that feelings, like lava, begin to lose their heat almost as soon as they overflow. After a time they cool to the point where they are no longer damaging or dangerous. You can explore an old lava flow on foot, though once it would have burned you.

WHEN TO DO IT

Try this self-soothing exercise every night for a month, or until your heartache has subsided. Time heals most emotional wounds, but this visualization might speed your way to recovery.

46 SWITCH THE LABELS

Here is an exercise to help you keep calm when dealing with tricky people. We all have to get along with people we find difficult—colleagues, in-laws, family members. The tools of cognitive behavioral therapy allow us to see the problem in a more helpful way. We may not be able to change those around us, but we can certainly change our reactions to them.

1 Think for a moment about the "labels" you attach to your tricky person: is he or she thoughtless? Condescending? Sarcastic? Imagine that word is written on a large label and attached to the person.

2 Now think about what labels this person might apply to you. Are they the same as the labels you would hope for? Imagine a label with your preferred word written on it, and imagine attaching it to yourself.

3 When you come into contact with this person, bring to mind your label. This allows you to recalibrate your expectations of yourself, and encourages you to assert yourself in healthier ways. And when the person is tricky, remember his or her label—remind yourself with a wry smile that you cannot change someone else.

WHEN TO DO IT

Do this exercise regularly. You will gradually become more adept at communicating from a position of determination rather than one of defensiveness. Shifting your own attitude may, little by little, encourage the other person to shift his or hers.

47 AMONG THE STARS

Do you find it hard to ask for help? Psychologists agree that having a shoulder to lean on when times get tough can help us calm down. According to emotional brain training, we need to make internal and external connections in order to reap the essential rewards of balance and intimacy. Use these three visualizations to remind yourself that talking to a friend can help empty your head of worries and your heart of pain.

1 As you pull back your blankets in the morning, take a long took at the tiny threads that are tightly woven together. Use this as an image to remind yourself that you are a part of the richly woven fabric of life.

2 In the afternoon take a walk and pay attention to the leaves on the trees. If they are waving, staying still, or falling down, use them to remind you that everyone is part of a wider whole.

3 In the evening look up at the sky and as you count the stars pay attention to how they twinkle. It's a reminder that your friends are out there and waiting for you to reach out.

WHEN TO DO IT

This is a three-part exercise that you can do every day. Spend a couple of minutes on each part for two weeks.

HOW TO HELP

Make eye contact with people you come into contact with, from colleagues to checkout clerks or waiting staff. By engaging fully with those we interact with, we become more aware of how much help we receive.

PERSONAL AFFIRMATION

can I see this situation in a **different** way?

48 TELLING TALES

Do you have a tendency to spin negative stories in your head? Many of us do, and these stories can get so entrenched in our thought processes that we start believing they are factual. Using the cognitive behavioral therapy tool of "gentle self-interrogation," you can learn to combat your negative thoughts before they lead to unnecessary conflict with others.

1 Get a pen and a piece of paper. Sit for a few moments, taking deep, calm breaths.

2 Ask yourself the questions below, using a kind inner voice:

What is really on my mind?
Is this fear being blown out of proportion?
Can I show myself this may not be the case?
Will this bother me in a few months' time?
Can I see this in any different way?

3 Write down your responses. Keep the paper somewhere to hand, and if your anxiety loop starts up again, refer back to what you wrote—this will help you to keep the anxieties down.

WHEN TO DO IT

If you have a tendency to be overwhelmed by your own narratives, try doing this exercise daily. Soon you will begin to see that your worries are often just figments of your stressed imagination, and you can gently let them go.

49 LET THE SUN SET

Try this loving visualization if you have a tendency to take your partner, or another family member, for granted. Our family relationships help us to feel calm and supported, but we need to release old stressors, appreciate the positive, and accept our differences to make the most of them.

1 Lie down on a couch and focus on breathing slowly in and out. With your eyes closed, imagine you are watching a stunning sunset. As the sun drops toward the horizon, you think about putting to rest all the regrets, resentments, grudges, blaming, and negativity you have stored up.

2 When the sun shuts down for the night, the stillness inside you allows you to think about the positives in your relationship, what you have accomplished together, and the blessings you have in your life right now.

3 Now open your eyes. Write down one thing you'll try to do to bring more contentment to your relationship—perhaps to compliment your partner every day, or to accept a trait that you struggle with.

WHEN TO DO IT

Try doing this once a week. By regularly revisiting what is good about our closest relationships, and letting go of the negatives, we can bring more calm into our homes and lives.

50 WALK OUT ANGER

It's normal to get angry sometimes. And when we do, just telling ourselves to calm down is unlikely to help. And yet we need to find a way to restore the equilibrium, to lower the emotional temperature. Cognitive behavioral therapy teaches us that we can use our bodies to gain control over our emotions, and release our feelings more healthily. Try these four ways.

1 Go for a brisk walk, jog, or run. If you can go somewhere beautiful, all the better.

2 Do some physical job, such as gardening or chopping wood. Even cleaning the bathroom or doing the vacuuming can be a good way to release some pent-up emotion.

3 Dance. Put on some up-tempo music and move to the beat.

4 Get creative. Drawing, painting, and coloring all help reduce stress, and are healthy ways for you to release anger.

Turn the page: try the coloring exercise overleaf

WHEN TO DO IT

Do this exercise when your anger feels disproportionate and seems likely to lead you to behave in ways you will regret. Working your body is a great way to center yourself once more.

PERSONAL AFFIRMATION TO COLOR

now I
enjoy a
sense of
peace
and
calm

ACKNOWLEDGMENTS

Picture credits 2–3 (and side detail throughout book) Incomible/Shutterstock 6 elwynn/ Shutterstock 9 Eric Gevaert/Shutterstock 11 Patrick Foto/Shutterstock 12–13 Transia Design/ Shutterstock 15 SJ Travel Photo and Video/Shutterstock 16 wenani/Shutterstock 18 Andrekart Photography/Shutterstock 20 Robynrg/Shutterstock 22 Jan Knop/Shutterstock 24 soulgems/ Shutterstock 26 Transia Design/Shutterstock 28 Yellowj/Shutterstock 30–31 Brian Kinney/ Shutterstock 32 iravgustin/Shutterstock 34 Yuganov Konstantin/Shutterstock 37 Letterberry/ Shutterstock 38–39 Kotkoa/Shutterstock 40–41 Julia Snegireva/Shutterstock 43 robert_s/ Shutterstock 44 Artyom Baranov/Shutterstock 47 Julia Snegireva/Shutterstock 48 S_Photo/ Shutterstock 50 elina/Shutterstock 52 jesadaphorn/Shutterstock 54 redd_pandda /Shutterstock 56 Julia Snegireva/Shutterstock 58–59 Roman Mikhailiuk/Shutterstock 60 Paisan Changhirun/ Shutterstock 62 pullia/Shutterstock 64 Julia Snegireva/Shutterstock 66 Katrina Elena/Shutterstock 69 Eskemar/Shutterstock 70–71 Afishka/Shutterstock 72–73 Transia Design/Shutterstock 75 Jes2u. photo/Shutterstock 76 leungchopan/Shutterstock 78 photokup/Shutterstock 80 yuri4u80/ Shutterstock 82 Transia Design/Shutterstock 84–85 KieferPix/Shutterstock 86 gn fotografie/ Shutterstock 88 Annaev/Shutterstock 90 Transia Design/Shutterstock 92 Chokniti Khongchum/ Shutterstock 94 Potapov Alexander/Shutterstock 95 Transia Design/Shutterstock 97 Snezh/ Shutterstock 98–99 Transia Design/Shutterstock 101 Ronald Sumners/Shutterstock 102 Labrador Photo Video/Shutterstock 104 WDG Photo/Shutterstock 106 Sari ONeal/Shutterstock 108 Ilya Akinshin/Shutterstock 110 Annette Shaff/Shutterstock 112 Ryszard Filipowicz/Shutterstock 114 EpicStockMedia/Shutterstock 115 Transia Design/Shutterstock 116 Plateresca/Shutterstock 118 nature photos/Shutterstock 120 Kochneva Tetyana/Shutterstock 122–123 Dmytro Balkhovitin/ Shutterstock 124 Triff/Shutterstock 126 Mega Pixel/Shutterstock 128 Sergii Votit/Shutterstock 130–131 facai/Shutterstock 132–133 Transia Design/Shutterstock 135 imging/Shutterstock 136 StevanZZ/Shutterstock 138 Transia Design/Shutterstock 140 Veniamin Kraskov/Shutterstock 142–143 Dmytro Balkhovitin/Shutterstock 144 Rainer Albiez/Shutterstock 146 B. and E. Dudzinscy/ Shutterstock 148 Albert Barr/Shutterstock 150 Transia Design/Shutterstock 152 Khoroshunova Olga/Shutterstock 154 MC2000/Shutterstock 156–157 Julia Snegireva/Shutterstock 158–159 Transia Design/Shutterstock

Cover: Incomible/Shutterstock

While every effort has been made to credit contributors, Quantum would like to apologize should there have been any omissions or errors, and would be pleased to make the appropriate corrections to future editions of the book.